MOMMY NEVER WENT TO HEBREW SCHOOL

Mindy Avra Portnoy
illustrated by Shelly O. Haas

KAR-BEN COPIES, INC.   ROCKVILLE, MD

Glossary

Afikomen:	Dessert matzah that is part of a seder hiding game designed to amuse young children
Dreidel:	Spinning top used in a Hanukkah game
Four Questions:	Asked by the youngest child at the Passover seder as an introduction to the Exodus story
Hanukkah:	Festival of Lights
Mezuzah:	A parchment with Hebrew prayers which is attached to the doorpost of a Jewish home
Mikveh:	Ritual bath
Passover seder:	Ritual meal celebrating the Exodus from Egypt
Shabbat:	Jewish Sabbath

Library of Congress Cataloging-in-Publication Data

Portnoy, Mindy Avra.
  Mommy never went to Hebrew school / Mindy Avra Portnoy; illustrated by Shelly O. Haas.
    p.   cm.
  Summary: A young boy discusses why and how his mother converted to Judaism before he was born.
  ISBN 0-930494-96-2 — ISBN 0-930484-97-0 (pbk.)
  /. Proselytes and proselyting. Jewish—Juvenile literature. (/. Judaism—Customs and practices.) I.
Haas, Shelly O., ill.
II. Title.
BM729.P7P57 1989
296.7' 1—dc19
                         89-30874
                              CIP
                              AC

Published by KAR-BEN COPIES, INC. Rockville, MD 1-800-4-KARBEN
Printed in the United States of America

To Philip

Jewish people are not all alike.

Some are tall, and some are short. Some live in cities, and some live in the suburbs. Some speak Hebrew, and some don't. And some grew up in Jewish families, and some didn't.

My mom, for example. She wasn't Jewish when she was little. Her mom and dad, my grandparents, are Christians—Presbyterians to be exact. When my mom was my age, she went to church on Christmas and Easter and sometimes on Sundays during the year.

I didn't figure this out until a couple of years ago, when I was six. I was home sick with the chicken pox and was moping around the house. Mom sent me to the big storage closet to check out the special "rainy day" toy box we keep there. All I could find were a sack of blocks and some picture books. Mom keeps forgetting I've outgrown all that. So I began exploring and discovered a box of old photos. Mom and dad looked so funny when they were little.

Mom always wore ribbons in her hair, and dad always wore a hat—sometimes a baseball hat, a cowboy hat, or a fireman's hat. Maybe he was bald then, too!

As I was looking through the box, I found a picture of mom sitting under a Christmas tree with a million presents around her. There were other pictures of her all dressed up, standing with her parents next to the tree.

I knew we always visited mom's family on Christmas day and brought them presents, but I guess I was just too little to wonder why my mom's parents had a Christmas tree and my dad's didn't.

I went downstairs and showed mom the pictures. She made us both a snack and told me about her conversion. That's when you start off not being Jewish when you're born, but become Jewish later on.

Mom said she was proud of her conversion but had waited to explain it to me. Parents sometimes forget that you usually figure things out before they think you're old enough to understand.

Mom explained that when she was about
my age, her best friend Lisa was Jewish.
Mom learned about Shabbat and Hanukkah,
and once even won a dreidel-spinning contest
at Lisa's house.

Mom met my dad in college. I think they winked at each other in history class and decided to get married. I winked at Rachel Miller the other day in math class, but she just giggled.

While they were getting to know each other, mom thought about becoming Jewish. Sometimes she went to synagogue with dad and his family. Later she started taking special classes with a rabbi.

She learned about the Jewish holidays and how to read some important prayers in Hebrew. When she studied Jewish history, she found out that Ruth in the Bible had chosen to become Jewish. Ruth was the great-grandmother of King David.

My name is David, too,
but I'm planning to be a
pilot, not a king.

Mom knew that becoming Jewish was an important decision, so she talked it over with her parents. They agreed that even though they might pray in different ways and celebrate different holidays, they could still love and respect each other.

When mom was converted, she met with three rabbis who asked her questions about being Jewish. Then she went into a special room with a mikveh. A mikveh is like a bathtub without any toys. She recited some prayers. Then she had to get all the way under the water, even her head.

Afterwards, mom's rabbi blessed her using her new
Hebrew name, and welcomed her as a member of the
Jewish people. He gave her a certificate and a
beautiful mezuzah for her door. Friends at the
synagogue made mom a party to celebrate.

A few months later, she and dad were married.
That all happened before I was born.

When mom first told me this, I wondered if I was the only Jewish kid whose mom wasn't always Jewish. Then I found out that Aaron's dad is also Jewish by choice, and Sharon's mom is, too. My friend Sarah told me that she went to the mikveh when she was a baby, because she was adopted by Jewish parents. But Sarah was so little that the rabbis didn't ask her any questions.

Last week, when I didn't feel like waking up for Hebrew School, I told mom I shouldn't have to go because she didn't have to when she was little. I thought it was a great argument.

But mom explained to me that she used to go to Sunday School classes at her church, and that she had to wake up even earlier.

I asked mom if anything would be different in her life if she had always been Jewish. She thought a minute, smiled, and said she was sorry she had never been the youngest at the Passover seder so she could ask the Four Questions.

Maybe I'll let her take my place this year...but I still want to find the afikomen all by myself.

ABOUT THE AUTHOR

Rabbi Mindy Avra Portnoy, a graduate of Yale University, was ordained at Hebrew Union College-Jewish Institute of Religion in New York, in 1980. She is currently Associate Rabbi at Temple Sinai in Washington, D.C. Rabbi Portnoy is the author of *Ima on the Bima: My Mommy is a Rabbi,* published by Kar-Ben Copies in 1986. She lives with her husband, Philip L. Breen, and their children, Ceala Eloise and Barney Samuel, in Kensington, Maryland.

ABOUT THE ILLUSTRATOR

Shelly O. Haas received her Bachelor of Fine Arts from The Rhode Island School of Design. Her commissions range from postage stamps to educational textbooks, and her interests from photography to herbal research. Her first book for Kar-Ben Copies, *Grandma's Soup,* was published earlier this year. Ms. Haas lives in Budd Lake, NJ, where she shares a studio with her husband.